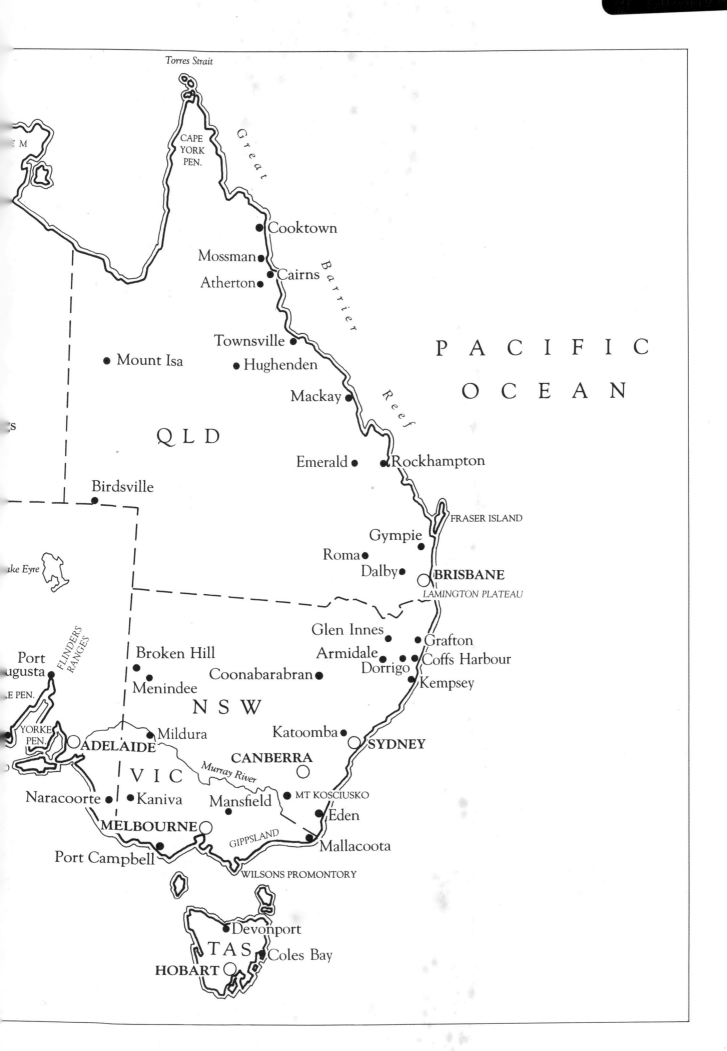

# Australia's
## NATIONAL PARKS
IMAGES AND IMPRESSIONS

June 94

To Mrs Zakalik,

   thankyou for a wonderful year!

With love and affection,

BuzzYSaLLie

Karri forest, Warren National Park, Western Australia

# AUSTRALIA'S
## NATIONAL PARKS
IMAGES AND IMPRESSIONS

## JOCELYN BURT

HOUGHTON MIFFLIN COMPANY

Boston   Melbourne

I would like to thank the following for their assistance with this book: Department of Conservation, Forests and Lands, Victoria; National Parks and Wildlife Service, New South Wales; National Parks and Wildlife Service, Queensland; National Parks and Wildlife Service, South Australia; Department of Conservation and Land Management, Western Australia; Department of Lands, Parks and Wildlife, Tasmania; Conservation Commission of the Northern Territory; Australian National Parks and Wildlife Service.

I would also like to thank Quicksilver Connections Ltd, Port Douglas, for the trip to the outer Great Barrier Reef; and Neil McLeod of Ningaloo Safari Tours, Exmouth, for the tour to Cape Range.

Most of the photographs for this book were taken with a Mamiya RB67 camera.

Houghton Mifflin Australia Pty Ltd
PO Box 97, Wantirna South, Victoria 3152
112 Lewis Rd, Wantirna South, Victoria 3152, Australia

Houghton Mifflin Company
2 Park St, Boston, Massachusetts 02108, USA

First published 1991
Text and photographs copyright © Jocelyn Burt 1991

National Library of Australia
Cataloguing-in-Publication entry:

Burt, Jocelyn.
  Australia's national parks.

  ISBN 0 86770 128 5.

  1. National parks and reserves — Australia. 2.
  National parks and reserves — Australia —
  Pictorial works. I. Title.

333.780994

US ISBN 0-395-49282-3
US CIP data is available

Edited by Alex Skovron
Designed by Noni Edmunds
Typeset in Bembo by Setrite Typesetters, Hong Kong
Printed in Singapore by Kyodo Printing Co. Ltd

# CONTENTS

Preface  7
Great Barrier Reef  10
Cape Hillsborough  12
Cooloola  14
Lamington  16
Natural Bridge  20
Daintree  22
Millstream Falls  26
Carnarvon  27
Bunya Mountains  28
Porcupine Gorge  29
Warrumbungle  30
Gibraltar Range  32
Hat Head  33
New England  34
Dorrigo  36
Mootwingee  38
Yuraygir  39
Blue Mountains  42
Kosciusko  44
Ben Boyd  47
Wilsons Promontory  48
Port Campbell  52
Croajingolong  55
Tarra-Bulga  56
Fraser  57
Alpine  60
Mount Buffalo  65
Grampians  66

Little Desert  68
Hattah-Kulkyne  69
Cradle Mountain - Lake St Clair  70
Southwest  76
Rocky Cape  79
Freycinet  80
Hartz Mountains  81
Lincoln  82
Naracoorte Caves  84
Innes  85
Mount Remarkable  87
Flinders Ranges  88
Flinders Chase  92
Uluru  94
Ormiston Gorge and Pound  98
Finke Gorge  99
Kakadu  100
Nitmiluk  106
Keep River  108
Gregory  109
Bungle Bungle  110
Windjana Gorge  114
Hamersley Range  116
Millstream-Chichester  119
Cape Range  122
Nambung  124
Walpole-Nornalup  125
Fitzgerald River  126
Eucla  128

Lake Eacham National Park, Queensland

# PREFACE

*For the use of the public forever as a national park...* In 1879 this important statement marked the initial dedication of 8600 hectares of bushland 23 kilometres south of Sydney which became the nucleus of the present Royal National Park, Australia's oldest. Seven years earlier a similar statement had been made by an American shortly before the creation of the world's first national park, Yellowstone, in the United States; in that country a number of people had been influenced by the writer Henry David Thoreau (1817–1862), who believed that the key to the preservation of the world lay in its wilderness areas. Today, his belief is loudly affirmed by many thousands worldwide, and most countries are now setting aside large tracts of land for national parks.

Since 1879 Australia has created more than 500 reserves to protect wilderness, notable scenery and landforms, fragile environments, and the habitats of endangered species of flora and fauna. More places are added each year. Some are given the status of national park, while others receive the lesser but nonetheless important classification of conservation park, nature park, State park, sanctuary, scenic reserve or wildlife reserve — the titles vary from State to State. A number of the national parks have been placed on the prestigious World Heritage List.

This book deals with Australia's national parks, although one conservation park, and the important Great Barrier Reef Marine Park, have been included. In sharing some of my impressions and experiences, I hope to give readers — and prospective travellers — a taste of what there is to see in some of the country's most popular parks and in a few of the not so well known ones. I also hope that readers will be inspired to discover many other aspects for themselves. Space limitations prevented the inclusion of every park, even of all the popular ones, and because the choice was so difficult I tended to select my favourite places (and even then there wasn't room for them all). The emphasis is very much on scenic beauty, which I believe is the prime attraction for most people. I have also chosen parks with relatively easy access for conventional two-wheel-drive vehicles (2WD), the exceptions being Bungle Bungle Range and Finke Gorge parks, where four-wheel-drive vehicles (4WD) are required; these two parks are so popular that many people without suitable cars take commercial tours instead.

During the 1980s there was a steady rise in the number of people visiting national parks — some of which were being described as 'loved to death': in danger of being destroyed by too many visitors. In order to cope with this increased volume of people and the resulting impact on the environment, park-management programs have had to undergo many changes. The changes have not always been welcomed, and there are those who believe that in a few parks the restrictions have become excessive. That may be so, but there is still a multitude of parks — even popular ones — that offer plenty of freedom and space where, in peace and solitude, you can delight in the wonders of nature that so gladden the heart and lift the soul.

Fitzroy Falls, Morton National Park, New South Wales

# GREAT BARRIER REEF

Stretching for 2000 kilometres along the east coast of Queensland, from Torres Strait in the north to Gladstone in the south, the Great Barrier Reef is a complex of innumerable coral reefs, cays, deepwater channels, bays, lagoons and rocky islands. Nearly all of this great masterpiece of nature is a marine park, and will eventually be the largest area set aside for conservation in the world. It has also been placed on the World Heritage List.

Although many of the islands are national parks in their own right, they are not part of the Great Barrier Reef Marine Park — but the coral reefs surrounding them are. A ranger explained that the islands are part of the State of Queensland, whereas the waters are under the jurisdiction of the Commonwealth; both are managed by the Queensland National Parks and Wildlife Service. Unlike land-based national parks, this marine park is a multi-use reserve, where everything from shell-collecting and fishing to shipping and tourist activities takes place (but not mining or oil-drilling — at the moment). For management purposes the Reef is divided into zones: General Use zone, where most activities are unrestricted; Marine National Park A zone, which caters for recreational pursuits; Marine Park B, a 'look but don't take' zone; and Preservation and Scientific zone, which covers small areas that are closed to the public.

For decades the most renowned place to sample the Great Barrier Reef has been Green Island, a small coral cay lying off Cairns. Boats travel daily from the mainland to the tourist resort, which occupies about one-third of the island, the rest being a national park. Here visitors can snorkel over the coral reef or take a glass-bottomed boat; there is also an underwater observatory and a marine museum.

At various locations, those who wish to see the outer reef can board fast catamarans to permanently based pontoons where they can view the coral and marine life from an underwater observatory or take a trip in one of the semi-submersible boats in which the actual viewing room is a couple of metres below the water; they can also go snorkelling or scuba-diving.

A trip to the outer reef is an unforgettable experience. Among my most memorable visits was that to Agincourt Reef, out from Port Douglas and one of the best places to see coral. There, a marine biologist from Reef Biosearch led a small group of us from the catamaran *Quicksilver* on a snorkelling tour of a section of the reef near the pontoon where the catamaran was moored. Like thousands before me, I discovered that you can't really appreciate the beauty of the reef until you have snorkelled in one of the lagoons — or better still, dived to deeper waters. It also adds to the interest if you know the names and the habits of the marine creatures you see — and that's another reason why the tour with the marine biologist, who identified many of the reef's life-forms for us, proved so enjoyable.

Aerial view of Green Island and its coral reef
Sooty terns nesting, Michaelmas Cay

QUEENSLAND

11

# CAPE HILLSBOROUGH

This delightful coastal park lies about 20 kilometres off the Bruce Highway, just north of Mackay. Here rugged hills drop steeply to the sea, and broad sandy beaches nestle between rocky headlands and lines of mangroves; walking-tracks pass through lowland forest, eucalypt woodlands, and hoop pines; and at the foot of Cape Hillsborough craggy boulders thrown from the volcanic Pinnacle Rock in an earlier era litter the beach.

It was along the Cape Hillsborough beach that I had the best walks, particularly at low tide when all the rocks were fully exposed. One of the most intriguing formations was a great tor that reared over the sand and looked remarkably like a man, although at a certain angle I thought it bore more resemblance to a dispirited sphinx; its official name is James Cook Head. At low tide, also, some rather unusual beauty appeared on the moist sand when thousands of sand-bubbler crabs created intricate patterns with masses of sandballs, left behind as they buried themselves. It seemed such a shame to walk on their handiwork.

Eastern grey kangaroos abounded in the park, many of them grazing peacefully around the foreshore and the nearby camping ground. Some campers said they had caught one of them raiding their tent for food. It also seemed that the roos liked to befriend visitors: one morning I spotted a big one contentedly loping beside a jogger. I wondered who was setting the pace.

James Cook Head

Cape Hillsborough

QUEENSLAND

# COOLOOLA

Situated between Rainbow Beach and Noosa Heads, 170 kilometres north of Brisbane, this park protects a wide variety of habitats, including heaths, swamps, lakes, dunes, eucalypt woodlands, the beautiful Noosa River, and some of Australia's most spectacular ocean beaches. Throughout the park most of the access is by 4WD, but commercial day tours are available that go from Noosa Heads and Tewantin up the Noosa River to the Kinaba Wetlands (which tour operators call the 'Everglades'), and to the Teewah Coloured Sands—the clifflike dunes of multicoloured sands lining Teewah Beach.

It is best to take the boat trip up the Noosa River on a day when there is no wind: the reflections will be superb, especially where the river narrows and the loose papery-barked melaleucas bend so low over the water that they appear to be on the verge of toppling in. Here the river is a tan colour, caused by water percolating through the upper sand-layer and picking up tannin and other chemicals from decaying vegetation. 'These chemicals make it almost like tea,' said the ranger at the Kinaba Information Centre. Unfortunately it was a windy day when I took the trip, though one corner of the river was sheltered enough to give some good reflections. The skipper said that on some days, when the surface was glassy and mirrored everything perfectly, it was like moving through space rather than water.

Access for private and tour-operated 4WDs to the Teewah Coloured Sands is by a vehicular ferry that crosses the Noosa River at Tewantin. Running for about 30 kilometres and in places rising to more than 60 metres, these incredible sands are relics of a system of iron-stained dunes that were deposited a long time ago when the sea-level was much lower. The sand is quite fragile and crumbles easily; the dunes are also at the mercy of the elements and are slowly receding. Fashioned by weather, they are shaped into canyons, bluffs and hills, and a mass of white sand lying in a red-and-orange canyon might appear remarkably like a miniature glacier.

There are more coloured dunes lining Rainbow Beach, in the northern part of the park. For walkers, there is easy access from the village of the same name, which lies beside the beach, and it takes about two hours to reach the end at Double Point. From the moment you set foot on the beach at the village, it is a lovely walk. The first time I did it, the outgoing tide had exposed many rocks that were just as colourful as the nearby dunes, and in the soft morning light of the rising sun their chunky shapes of black and gold, with others wearing green seaweed, were wonderfully accentuated. But on my next visit, some years later, I was disappointed to find that not a rock was visible on the beach. Apparently a storm will often bring in sand that covers the rocks, and then another may sweep it all away again. A notice nearby confirmed this by advising motorists that exposed rocks may at times prevent access to Double Point.

Rainbow Beach
'Everglades', Noosa River

# LAMINGTON

Queensland's most popular national park and one of my firm favourites, Lamington covers much of Lamington Plateau, set high in the Great Dividing Range and bordered by escarpments rising to over 900 metres. It is on the south side of the Scenic Rim — the crescent of mountains lying behind Brisbane. The plateau is also known as Green Mountains, a name given to the locality around the year 1900. The park protects an outstanding area of undisturbed subtropical rainforest containing some remnant vegetation from a cooler era, the most notable species being the ancient Antarctic beech trees. There is also much beauty here in its streams, waterfalls and gorges, and from the plateau edges breathtaking panoramas sweep to the coast and over the ranges.

There are two access-points to the park: Binna Burra on the north-east side of the plateau, and O'Reillys in the west. Both have a lodge and camping ground from where a network of walking-paths radiate into the wilderness of the park, the main one being the 22-kilometre Border Track which links the two places. I have heard of hikers who complete this return route — one of Australia's loveliest forest walks — in a day, which means they must travel through the forest like greyhounds in training with little time to drink in the charm of the vegetation and the views. A better way is to be at one of the lodges when it takes its guests to the other side of the mountain for the day: those who choose to walk the Border Track instead of being driven around will be picked up at the end of the day.

It is along the Border Track that those wonderful Methuselahs of the forest, the Antarctic beeches, are to be found. Growing only in the high parts of the plateau, these relics of an ice age are among the finest and oldest in the Southern Hemisphere. Nobody has been able to say with certainty just how old they are, but forestry experts think the older ones could be at least 3000 years. They certainly look incredibly old, with their robes of green moss covering gnarled and knobbly trunks that sometimes form caverns, their walls looking as if they could crumble at the slightest touch. Some *are* disintegrating, while other sturdy ones are so huge that they resemble fairytale fortresses; all have tremendous character and are at their most alluring when enveloped in fog.

In the past I have preferred to stay at O'Reillys — despite experiencing difficulties with my campervan in a muddy, steep-sloped camping ground — because O'Reillys is nearer to the best Antarctic beeches, and I have a particular love for the Box Forest Circuit (once called the Garden of Giants because of its many big trees) and for the Tooloona Track with the exquisite Elebana Falls. On my last trip, however, although I already had some knowledge of the Binna Burra side, I decided to explore it more fully and found so many beautiful places that I am now hard pressed to state which is my favourite part of Lamington. I also gave the camping ground a miss and stayed at the excellent Binna Burra Lodge, which offers much more than just a place to rest overnight. What with the variety of walks and the interesting activities organized by the lodge staff, I ended up staying longer than planned.

Tullawallal Circuit Track, near Binna Burra

Antarctic beech (*Nothofagus moorei*), Border Track, near O'Reillys

Elebana Falls, near O'Reillys

# NATURAL BRIDGE

This is another park in south-east Queensland's Scenic Rim. Lying in the McPherson Range, which forms part of the border between Queensland and New South Wales, it is named after its main attraction: Natural Bridge, an eroded roof of a cave through which pours Cave Creek. For years confusion has reigned over its name. The original title was Natural Bridge, but because tourists called it an arch it was renamed Natural Arch; this so upset the locals that the earlier name was restored.

It had been fifteen years since my last visit and I had forgotten how lovely this park was. I was not alone in enjoying its beauty: a steady stream of visitors walked the splendid one-kilometre circuit track that leads from the picnic-ground to the creek and bridge. Access is easy as the park lies close to the Nerang–Chillingham road.

Another superb place in the park is the Best of All Lookout, an aptly named viewing area set high on the Springbrook Plateau. Situated near Springbrook and giving aerial-like vistas over the ranges, the lookout is at the end of a short walk that passes through rainforest, with some fine stands of Antarctic beech. Many years ago I spent a winter's night in the 950-metre-high carpark and nearly died of cold — but the discomfort was forgotten when, from the lookout, I watched the early-morning light break magically over the ranges.

Natural Bridge

View from the Best of All Lookout

# DAINTREE

Lying behind the sugar town of Mossman in far north Queensland, Daintree National Park protects the impressive Main Coast Range, a part of the Great Divide. Much of this wild area of scarps, rugged tablelands and deep valleys is covered by dense tropical rainforest that provides a haven for many birds and animals, including tree-kangaroos and golden bowerbirds. Rain, clouds and mist prevail over these mountains, and the annual rainfall is so heavy that it can be measured in metres. All this moisture feeds the headwaters of many rivers and creeks, including the Daintree River, a major watercourse rising on the Windsor Tableland; further to the south is the Mossman River, a relatively short stream that has carved a deep gorge in the south-east corner of the park. Although this wilderness park is mostly inaccessible except to experienced and hardy bushwalkers, the lower end of Mossman Gorge is easy to reach and, since it lies just five kilometres from Mossman, has become a popular spot with both locals and tourists.

From the carpark, a short walking-track leads through lowland rainforest to several enchanting spots by the river, including a quiet pool suitable for swimming (the water is surprisingly cold). The river upstream is studded with boulders and whitewater rapids which give it great character and offer some good exploring if you don't mind boulder-hopping. I watched a strong young man swimming in the rapids area while the loudly gurgling water tumbled over him, and over the rocks, like miniature waterfalls. The swimmer later admitted that he had found the rapids too strong for comfort: 'I felt as if I was in a washing machine,' he said. Just as I was thinking what a dangerous place for inexperienced swimmers this could be, an elderly lady in a tour group slipped on the steep rocks beyond the end of the cement pathway and had to be carried out, with a possible broken leg. I noticed her shoes, and it wasn't surprising that she had fallen: they were dainty, slippery-soled sandals more suitable for a lounge-room than for exploring rugged boulders.

Mossman River

QUEENSLAND

23

Rapids, Mossman River

# MILLSTREAM FALLS

Set in open eucalypt woodland, the Millstream Falls lie on the drier western side of the Atherton Tableland behind Cairns in north Queensland, six kilometres from Ravenshoe and just off the Mount Garnet road. The main feature of this small park is the falls, which are reputed to be Australia's widest, spreading up to 100 metres across the rocky escarpment after heavy rains. A favourite with visitors, the cascade always presents a pleasing spectacle, even in the dry season when many other falls in the region are reduced to a trickle. From the carpark there is easy walking to viewing areas along the hillside, and a path leads down to the base of the falls and a large pool that is ideal for swimming.

Millstream Falls

# CARNARVON

Lying about 760 kilometres to the north-west of Brisbane between Roma and Emerald on the Consuelo Tableland, the main feature of this park is Carnarvon Gorge, a great chasm of towering sandstone that reaches heights of 180 metres. The gorge, which runs for 32 kilometres and shelters Carnarvon Creek — and a host of plants, including ferns, mosses, palms and ancient cycads — can be explored only on foot. Based on old cattle tracks, the main path follows the creek, crossing it many times; other tracks run off it to numerous side gorges, such as Violet Gorge, the Moss Gardens and the Hell Hole. 'Leave nothing but footprints, take nothing but photographs' was the park's motto in 1971, when I made my first visit. In those days you would probably have had the camping ground to yourself; today it is so popular you have to book a site in advance. There is also a lodge situated three kilometres from the gorge, just outside the park.

Carnarvon Gorge

# BUNYA MOUNTAINS

Queensland's second-oldest park after Tamborine Mountain, Bunya Mountains was gazetted in 1908. Today we can appreciate this important decision, because the Bunya pine was milled so extensively in the nineteenth century that this is now the only area where natural Bunya pine forests still stand. These mountains are an isolated section of the Great Dividing Range, and lie 55 kilometres north of Dalby in south-eastern Queensland. A network of walking-tracks crisscrosses the park, leading to waterfalls, gorges and lookouts over the Darling Downs. I loved it here, and often repeated some of the walks just to see once more the magnificent pines whose trunks soared so dramatically into the rainforest's high canopy.

Bunya pine (*Araucaria bidwillii*)

# PORCUPINE GORGE

I had never heard of this park until a fellow-traveller I met insisted I should see it the next time I passed through north-west Queensland. Because the road to it was not sealed, I checked its condition at Hughenden police station, 64 kilometres south of the park. After confirming that it was suitable for 2WDs, I asked the policeman what the gorge was like. 'It's just a dirty big hole in the ground,' he said. Knowing that the National Parks and Wildlife Service isn't usually interested in protecting dirty big holes in the ground, I pressed him further and asked if it was scenic. 'I suppose so,' he shrugged, 'if you like that sort of thing.'

Well, it was *very* scenic; in fact it was a fantastic place. I took the road to the main lookout and with considerable astonishment beheld a great canyon that yawned open in the sparsely-wooded dry plains. Vertical cliffs plunged a good 100 metres to the stream below, and the calls of myriad birds reverberated throughout the gorge, which runs for 20 kilometres. As I walked along the clifftops in a southerly direction the scenes became grander, with the gorge deepening and the walls growing more sheer. Although it was the peak of the winter tourist season, nobody was around.

Porcupine Gorge

# WARRUMBUNGLE

Many motorists have their first glimpse of the remarkable Warrumbungle Range from the Newell Highway. Once they see the distinctive spires and domes topping its heights, visitors are easily beckoned to make the 32-kilometre detour from Coonabarabran to explore it. There is also access via the Coonamble road, which enters the national park on its western side, but this route may include some very rough gravel sections whereas the road from Coonabarabran is sealed. The Warrumbungles, as the range is often called, lie about 500 kilometres north-west of Sydney.

The spires and domes are plugs of the last cooling lava that formed in the cores of dying volcanoes at the end of a particularly active volcanic era in ages past. The most unusual is the Breadknife, a straight wall of rock nearly 100 metres high and only about a metre thick. The formations, particularly Belougery Spire and Crater Bluff, are very popular with rock-climbers—there is even a visitors' book to sign at the top of Belougery Spire, which is classed as a relatively easy climb for the initiated (though for non-climbers it looks anything but!). Climbing the Breadknife is banned, however, because the rock, fractured by frequent severe frosts, breaks away very easily and is dangerous both for climbers and for those walking below.

There are some excellent walks in the park but everybody's favourite is the one that leads to the Grand High Tops, passing the base of the Breadknife before it reaches the top ridge with its outstanding views. When I first did this four-hour return walk I reached the ridge of the Grand High Tops around midday and found the lighting for photography disappointing, because I was shooting slightly into the sun. On my next visit, therefore, I decided that the only time to be at the top was at sunrise—which meant walking for more than an hour in the dark forest. As there was no moon it was rather spooky until the first light began to filter through the trees, and I tried not to think too much about a passing comment someone had breezily made to me before this visit: 'That's Yowie country in the Warrumbungles!' The Yowie is Australia's version of the Yeti, the mythical Himalayan creature that resembles a large primate.

Another walk I found rewarding at sunrise was the Alex Gould Circuit, which was easier on the leg muscles. It took only a little over an hour to reach the top of Macha Tor from the Pincham carpark. The final scramble up to the summit of the tor was a bit difficult as my backpack with all the camera equipment barely fitted between the walls of the narrow ravine that served as a track. But the sight of the first rays of the sun lighting up the towering spires on the Grand High Tops was glorious.

View to the Grand High Tops, from the Alex Gould Circuit
Belougery Spire, from the Grand High Tops

# GIBRALTAR RANGE

Set high on a forested plateau at the edge of the New England Tablelands, this park lies about halfway between Glen Innes and Grafton, beside the Gwydir Highway, in north-east New South Wales. Many granite tors stud the area, and there are some fine lookouts, waterfalls and heathlands rich in wildflowers—this is a good place to see the showy waratahs. I always enjoy the three-kilometre walk from Mulligans Hut camping ground to the Needles, a collection of enormous boulders rearing above the treetops of the 900-metre escarpment. Crossing the planks that serve as a bridge over the river near the camping ground can be tricky if the river is in spate: the last time I was there the swift-moving water spilled over the bridge, causing the surface to be fearsomely slippery.

The Needles

# HAT HEAD

It was this park's curious name which initially lured me to explore it. Although the conical headland of Hat Head didn't strike me as looking much like a hat, I was amazed to find here one of the most dramatic stretches of dunes to be seen along the east coast. It is also one of the few great sandy areas to have escaped the ravages of sandmining. The national park lies close to the small village of Hat Head, 21 kilometres east of Kempsey on the north coast of New South Wales.

I camped at the Hungry Rest Area, an attractive camping ground that nestles into the edge of the dunes. Apart from a mob of kangaroos looking as if they were happy to make friends provided food was on offer, the place was almost deserted. But this may have been unusual: a notice advised campers that they were not to stay for more than six weeks! Apparently it is a favourite place with fishermen who fish off the beach, to which there is access only by a 4WD track or a long walk over the dunes from the Hungry Rest Area. I was content to explore the dunes from the camping ground, and to take the relatively short but delightful walk around Hat Head and Connors Hill.

Dunes near the Hungry Rest Area

# NEW ENGLAND

It had been twelve years since my last visit and I was pleased to find little change in this superb national park that lies near the Armidale–Dorrigo road in northern New South Wales. Situated above 1400 metres on the New England Plateau where its eastern edges end abruptly with steep escarpments and densely forested ridges falling to valleys of the Bellinger River system, New England National Park receives plenty of rainfall in summer and is extremely cold in winter. Although it is a popular place with day visitors, especially at weekends, I suspect its high altitude puts many people off camping there: even in September and May, I have experienced temperatures of around 0°C with biting winds, and there is no electricity to plug into in the bush camp set near the 1563-metre-high Point Lookout (though there is some cabin accommodation available in the park). In mid-winter it can be cold enough for Weeping Rock, which lies just below Point Lookout, to be coated in ice.

It may be a cold place, but it provides some good and sometimes strenuous walking on steep tracks that pass through cool temperate rainforest and gullies of lush treeferns. There are some splendid lookouts, the best being at Point Lookout, only a few minutes from the top carpark. An excellent walk is the Eagles Nest track, which starts at the Point Lookout carpark. The round trip takes about an hour and three-quarters, and includes Weeping Rock, Rainbow Spray, the Eagles Nest lookout and other viewing areas; the track also passes through some spacious rainforest where stands of Antarctic beech trees, their old and gnarled limbs draped in green mosses and ribbons of lichen, give the forest a cathedral-like atmosphere. There are some steep grades on this route, but it *is* worth the effort. If you are short of time (or energy), there is a small carpark below Point Lookout, from where it is only a ten-minute walk to Weeping Rock.

On my last visit I decided to do the Cascades walk, a round trip of seven kilometres starting near the park entrance. It was only 6°C on that May morning when I set off after breakfast, so it took a while to warm up walking in the cool of the forest. Unfortunately I never finished the walk: shortly before reaching the Cascades I suddenly noticed that the track was barely definable, and then it just disappeared. All at once the forest lost its enchantment: instead it became threatening and almost seemed to close in on me in the gloomy light. This vast forest wilderness was no place to be without a clear track, so I turned back.

From Point Lookout

NEW SOUTH WALES

# DORRIGO

For travellers wishing to cross the Great Dividing Range from west to east (or the other way) in northern New South Wales, there are various routes from which to choose. A favourite of mine is the Armidale–Bellingen road, which passes a number of national parks. One of these is Dorrigo, lying by the highway a few kilometres from the town of Dorrigo. The park protects the wild and rugged escarpment of the Dorrigo Plateau, and a variety of walking-tracks meander through the rainforest, passing large trees (including some monster-sized stumps marked with axemen's notches from an earlier logging period) and waterfalls that yield to views over forested valleys.

The last time I was there it rained all day, and although the wet conditions along the track to the Casuarina Falls were not ideal for walking or for the camera, the ambience of the forest was marvellous. Wet leaves glistened and damp stones shone; recently cut logs cleared from the track displayed a red grain made richer in colour by the moisture, which caused it almost to glow in the green gloom of the forest; and the valleys and forest-clad slopes viewed from clearings were steaming with mists. Not so marvellous were the leeches that made their presence felt in the wet conditions; worse, I even carried some back on my clothes and for the next twenty-four hours kept finding them on the march throughout my campervan.

Forest near the Never Never Picnic Area

From Casuarina Falls

NEW SOUTH WALES

37

# MOOTWINGEE

One of the most interesting national parks of New South Wales, Mootwingee is situated 130 kilometres north-east of Broken Hill. Breathing the very essence of timelessness and antiquity, its series of valleys between domed, eroded hills of sandstone in the Bynguano Range contain a wealth of Aboriginal art and relics. It is also home for most of the State's remaining population of yellow-footed rock-wallabies. Throughout the park there is evidence of weathering in the rocks, but to my mind nowhere is the result more astonishing than at Mushroom Rock, an eroded piece of sandstone rising from the ground like a colourful toadstool.

Mushroom Rock

# YURAYGIR

I discovered this park on an occasion when I was looking for a suitable place other than a coastal caravan park to camp overnight. Yuraygir's Station Creek was so appealing that I ended up staying for two days. Situated on the far north coast of New South Wales, Yuraygir National Park is fragmented into three sections lying between Yamba in the north and Red Rock in the south. Station Creek is in the most southern section, some 40 kilometres north of Coffs Harbour. It is one of the quietest camping grounds in the park, because access from the Pacific Highway is via ten kilometres of unsealed forest road that in parts looks as if it could be extremely slippery after rain. It was a weekend when I was there yet very few people came in.

Near my camp among fine stands of banksias and rusty gums, a sign advised 'Steps To Creek'. Thinking it would be just an ordinary bush stream, I wandered down without the camera; but after taking one look at the scene, I raced back for it in order to capture the splendid light over the large dune reflecting in the creek — which was more like a lagoon — that now glowed in the dusk. It was a beautiful place, particularly at sunrise and sunset. I spent much of the weekend exploring the expanse of sand that lined part of the estuary and backed the surf beach.

Station Creek after sunset

Sunrise over Station Creek

# BLUE MOUNTAINS

Named for the particular hue they take on when viewed from a distance — a colour caused by particles of vaporized eucalyptus oil scattering blue light — the rugged Blue Mountains contain some of Australia's most photographed landscapes. The park lies between two other national parks: Wollemi to the north, and Kanangra-Boyd to the south-west, together forming one of the largest protected natural areas in New South Wales. Part of the Great Dividing Range, these mountains are in fact an 1100-metre-high sandstone plateau spectacularly dissected by a number of rivers, one being the Grose River, which has cut a valley 760 metres deep. As a result, the grand scenery is viewed from the edges of the plateau, and anyone wishing to explore the valleys below must descend on foot. However, if you don't feel like taking the hard walks down to the bottom, there are some much easier ones around the plateau's rim, especially from Blackheath, and from Bells Line of Road on the other side of the valley.

Because the park is only 100 kilometres west of Sydney and borders numerous settlements (including the bustling town of Katoomba) that are strung along the Great Western Highway, it is an extremely popular place. I always find it an enormous relief to escape to the park's walking-tracks after negotiating the highway's heavy traffic, which gives the impression that the region is an extension of Sydney's western suburbs (some people will tell you it is). Indeed, once on the tracks it is hard to believe that suburbia lies almost nearby; one sad reminder is the notices that advise visitors to carry their own drinking-water as pollution has rendered the local stream water unfit for drinking.

The main area for walkers is the Grose Valley, just east of Blackheath. Many people take the two-hour return walk down to the base of the Bridal Falls, below Govetts Leap. The track is steep and seems to have been gouged into the almost knife-sheer mountainside, as has the multitude of steps that mark the path for most of the way down — though in one spot the steps become a metal stairway, attached to the cliff but rather unnervingly giving the sensation that it is hanging in mid-air. In places there is often so much moisture seeping from the cliffs that it forms a fine curtain of spray, dampening the path and anyone on it. Down and down goes the track, growing steeper, as do the steps, and you try not to think of the upward journey; but the wonderful views over the Grose Valley make it all worthwhile. By now the vegetation is lusher and the air noticeably warmer than at the top, and once you reach the base of the falls it is good to sit and rest while drinking in the beauty of the scene. If there is a wind blowing, photographers may have a frustrating time trying to capture the waterfall on film: the long wispy ribbon of water is easily blown to the side, and just as you are about to shoot it can move out of the picture.

Govetts Leap, with the Bridal Falls at far right

NEW SOUTH WALES

# KOSCIUSKO

This important alpine park covers a good portion of the Snowy Mountains in the Australian Alps, the country's highest landmass, which rises in wild splendour in the Great Dividing Range. The largest in New South Wales, the park extends south from Tumut and the national capital, Canberra, to the Victorian border; it also adjoins Victoria's Alpine National Park, and Namadgi National Park in the Australian Capital Territory. Between them, the three parks span a vast portion of mainland Australia's alpine area.

Although the Snowy Mountains Hydro-electric Scheme and a number of ski resorts intrude into the park, at least half of it is true wilderness, where landscapes and vegetation are virtually in their natural state. There are many summits over 2100 metres, including Australia's highest mountain, Mount Kosciusko, at 2228 metres; but few of the heights have grand peaks, since most of the elevated areas consist of broad plains and relatively gentle slopes dotted with broken chunky granite and glacial lakes. With an altitude range of up to 1800 metres within the park, there is a wide variety of habitats. One of the loveliest drives through the park is via the Alpine Way, which runs from the low country at Khancoban, up through some fine eucalypt forests, to Tom Groggin where the mighty Murray River is a young stream, and then on to Thredbo.

Of all the walks, the most popular is to the summit of Mount Kosciusko. There are two routes: from Charlotte Pass by the old road (now closed), and the shorter five-kilometre route from Thredbo, first taking the chairlift to the top and walking across from there. During summer weekends the Thredbo track can be packed with walkers, and it's wise to start early if you want to enjoy some solitude for at least the outward journey. I did this one Sunday, but by the time I had started to walk back the track was streaming with people. It was a warm day, but a change had been forecast and already clouds were building up. Despite this, many walkers setting off in the afternoon took no extra clothing—the only item one very scantily clad fellow carried was a packet of cigarettes! As in all alpine areas, the weather can change quickly, and can even bring snow at the height of summer. If it is warm down in the valley at the start of the walk, don't rely on the same temperature at the summit.

One necessary conservation measure taken on the Thredbo track to combat the erosion caused by constant use is the placing of a raised metal walkway over the original path for much of the route. When it was first constructed it was quite an eyesore, and it also clanked and clattered as you walked over it. But on my last visit I was glad to see that the ground underneath and beside it had revegetated well and in places grass was actually pushing through the iron grid. This regrowth had produced a softening effect and the walkway no longer seemed such a blot on the landscape; nor was it as noisy to walk on. Given more time, it may blend well into the terrain.

Murray River at Tom Groggin
Snow gums (*Eucalyptus pauciflora*), Charlotte Pass

NEW SOUTH WALES

Granite tors, Kosciusko Walk

# BEN BOYD

When a national park lies close to a highway and the access to it is easy, it is a shame not to take time to explore it—you never know what delights it may contain. Such a park is Ben Boyd, situated in the far-south-east corner of New South Wales, close to Eden. It comprises two areas that flank Twofold Bay, where in the nineteenth century the merchant Ben Boyd ran his famous whaling activities while hoping to create around the bay a city that would rival Sydney.

Apart from the area's interesting history, the park features long sandy beaches, sheltered coves and tranquil inlets, cliffs and headlands, dune scrubs and heathlands. The northern section of the park offers one of the most colourful sights along the entire south-eastern coast of the continent: the Quorabaragun Pinnacles, an extraordinarily eroded gully of soft white sandstone capped with red gravelly clay. The Pinnacles carpark is only a few minutes' drive from the Princes Highway, and there are good views over the Pinnacles, and over South Long Beach, from the kilometre-long walking-track that loops back to the carpark. There is also access to the beach from this track.

Quorabaragun Pinnacles

# WILSONS PROMONTORY

Whenever I am asked which is my favourite place in Australia, Wilsons Promontory is one of several that come to mind. My affection for the Prom — as it is often called by Victorians — began in the 1970s, and over the years, after countless visits and some pretty gruelling hikes, the place is firmly entrenched in my heart.

Situated in south Gippsland, 225 kilometres south-east of Melbourne, this high granite peninsula pushes into the cold waters of Bass Strait to form the most southerly point of the Australian mainland. It has that marvellous combination of mountain and sea, and behind the long wide beaches lying between bold granite headlands, there are eucalypt forests that give way to wildflower-rich heaths and sheltered gullies hiding treeferns, moss-covered rocks and sparkling streams. Granite is everywhere and largely contributes to the Prom's strength and character. Hills, peaks and headlands are strewn with tors of astonishing shapes and sizes or studded with massive slabs that fall away as sheer cliffs to the often turbulent sea. Even the weather, which can turn quite wild and stormy, gives the place a tremendous moodiness and a stirring beauty. Visitors sometimes despair of the climate, particularly in spring, but it is the cooler, blustery days which are so good for walking. The most stable months are in late summer and early autumn.

The base for visitors is Tidal River at Norman Bay, where a holiday resort provides camping facilities and lodges. Most of the Prom's scenic spots are accessible only by walking-tracks, and one of the joys of this national park is that there are plenty of short, easy walks, as well as longer and more challenging hikes. Of all the long day walks, the one to Sealers Cove is probably the most popular. This track starts and ends at the Mount Oberon carpark and is part of the famous circuit route that links Sealers and Refuge coves and Waterloo Bay. To walk this 37-kilometre circuit is, for me, the ultimate experience at Wilsons Promontory. Most people take two or three days to complete the walk, camping at the various outstations allocated along the track. The majority of the coves are safe for swimming, but not Waterloo Bay — as I learnt the hard way. Having thought it safe to splash around at the water's edge, I was most alarmed to find a strong undertow dragging me towards the open sea. I had considerable difficulty in getting out.

For the fit, the circuit is a relatively easy walk now that all the swamps have been spanned by boardwalks. When I first did the circuit, the swamps behind Waterloo Bay were a maze of vague tracks meandering through a jungle of paperbarks and a soft black mud that was knee-deep in places. Confused footprints went in all directions, my backpack kept tangling in the trees, and when I clutched a clump of sword-grass in order to regain my balance after floundering in the mud, it was like grabbing a handful of knives. To add to my misery it was one of those rare occasions when the mercury soared to 38°C. After I was out of the swamps and resting in the spindly shade of a small tree, four young men who had been behind me appeared and collapsed nearby. 'To think we took sickies for *this!*' one of them gasped.

The summit, Mount Oberon

Soft treefern (*Dicksonia antarctica*), Lilly Pilly Gully

VICTORIA

Dunes, Oberon Bay

# PORT CAMPBELL

It is hardly surprising that this national park receives a huge number of visitors, for it provides easy access to some of the world's most dramatic and thrilling coastal scenery. Stretching for 32 kilometres along the coast east of Warrnambool, the park lies off the western end of the Great Ocean Road, where the plains of the Western District abruptly give way to sheer limestone cliffs that plunge into the Southern Ocean. These cliffs are riddled with tunnels, caves and blowholes, and some of the headlands have been worn over the ages into archways and natural bridges by the ocean's powerful waves; in places whole sections have broken off to form islands and rocky stacks. Many vessels have been wrecked off this coast, which is still regarded as a most perilous area for shipping. One of the coastal gorges was named after the clipper *Loch Ard*, which foundered in the gorge in 1878 with the loss of 50 lives.

Port Campbell has been described as a shoreline in retreat, and one that is being constantly fashioned by the strong forces of nature. This was clearly demonstrated on a summer evening in January 1990, when one of the park's most famous landforms, London Bridge, collapsed into the sea leaving a new, orphan stack standing offshore. The spectacular crash of the great limestone mass sent a 25-metre-high column of water rearing into the sky, and left two tourists stranded on what had suddenly become an island;

after a cold wait for nearly three hours in a howling south-westerly, they were plucked to safety by a helicopter rescue crew. One trembles to think about the coachloads of tourists who had often lined up across the bridge while someone on the opposite cliff took photographs. After the collapse rangers were plied with many questions, the commonest being whether the national parks staff would rebuild the bridge, and whether people walking over it had contributed to its fall. The rangers would patiently explain how this coast is being eroded all the time, and remind the tourists that the most famous landforms in the park, the Twelve Apostles, were themselves once joined to the mainland.

Situated east of the small town of Port Campbell, the Twelve Apostles are a series of craggy stacks of varying shapes and sizes which tower grandly over the surf and a long sandy beach lying beside the vertical cliffs. The view from the clifftop near the road is one of Australia's best-loved panoramas. Walking-paths used to meander in all directions around the clifftops, but now a boardwalk has been built to protect the environment. This, of course, is necessary because of the large number of people coming here; but although it is an excellent boardwalk, I was rather saddened to see it, as visitors must now stick to it rather than wandering off where they like.

London Bridge before its collapse
. . . and after January 1990

Twelve Apostles beach

# CROAJINGOLONG

East Gippsland is one of Victoria's most scenic regions, so it is fitting that a national park should protect a good portion of its coastline. Stretching for about 100 kilometres from Sydenham Inlet to the New South Wales border, Croajingolong is a favourite with naturalists because of the wide variety of habitats that contain a wealth of wildflowers, including some rare species. The picturesque Mallacoota Inlet provides the easiest base for exploring the park.

A number of roads give access to other parts, but many are only 4WD tracks. Two interesting places, Thurra River and Wingan Inlet, are accessible for 2WDs if there hasn't been too much rain—it is always wise to check first at the park office at Cann River. Thurra River lies 38 kilometres south of Cann River. On my first visit I had no idea what to expect, and as there was no hint of beauty until I turned the last corner just before the bridge, it was a treat to confront the splendid scene—of the Thurra River dominated by a high dune—that suddenly opened up ahead, upstream of the river; downstream, a sandbar lay across its mouth. At the nearby camping ground the only sounds came from the surf breaking on the beach and the twittering of many birds in the banksia trees.

Thurra River

# TARRA-BULGA

In the 1980s two small parks, Tarra Valley and Bulga, little more than pockets lying in south Gippsland's Strzelecki Ranges, were amalgamated. When one considers the history of land-clearing in these ranges, it is quite miraculous that the two parks, with their giant mountain-ash trees, ancient myrtle-beeches and treeferns, have escaped the axe and the ravages of bushfires. From the picnic area at Tarra Valley, a forty-minute walking-path loops through the forest to Cyathea Falls, passing by shady rock-strewn streams and through the loveliest groves of treeferns I have seen anywhere in Australia.

Tarra Valley

# FRASER

Most Victorians have heard of Lake Eildon, near Mansfield, but not so many seem to know that Fraser National Park lies beside it. A manmade reservoir, the lake was created in the 1950s by the damming of the Goulburn River, which flooded forests and quite a few farms. Soon afterwards the park was established on the western shore, taking in former grazing land of the hilltops and slopes above the new lake's water-level. Right from the start regeneration of the grazing land was encouraged, and continues today: in 1990 about 9000 trees were planted, all being indigenous species grown from seed collected in the park.

There is ample space for camping by the lake, but in summer it is wise to book. Many people come for watersports, but for others like myself the drawcard is the views of the lake and surrounding hills; at sunrise the place is glorious. Many of the walks are up steep slopes that will surely test your muscles and fitness, but the landscapes make it worthwhile. However, the scenic trail that winds around the lake from Wallaby Bay to Cook Point is an easy one. One evening at Wallaby Bay I was busily taking photographs when I suddenly had the feeling I was not alone: sure enough, to the left were five wide-eyed eastern grey kangaroos, standing upright like soldiers in a line and gazing at me in astonishment. They looked so comical that I laughed, which of course sent them hopping off.

Devil Cove, from the camping ground

Lake Eildon

# ALPINE

Covering an immense area of high country stretching along the Great Dividing Range from near Mansfield and Licola to the New South Wales border, Alpine National Park was created in 1989 by the amalgamation of some crown land around Dartmouth Dam with three existing parks: Wonnangatta-Moroka, just north-east of the Jamieson—Heyfield road; Cobberas-Tingaringy, in the far corner of east Gippsland; and Bogong, part of the Victorian Alps where the State's highest peak, Mount Bogong, rises to 1986 metres. One of the park's major features for hikers is the Alpine Walking Track, which crosses the park and forms the base route for a system of other trails.

I live in the Ovens Valley in north-east Victoria, so this parks lies virtually at my back door. What a delight it is in summer to drive friends up to the Bogong High Plains for walks and to see the wildflowers; or at the end of a fine day to decide suddenly to take a picnic tea up to a spot near Mount Loch or Mount Feathertop and watch the sun set over a vast sea of folded ranges lying below, all bathed in misty mauves, each ridge a slightly different shade. Come winter, the snow beckons and there is the joy of loading the car with cross-country skis (and cameras) for a day's outing in a magical white wonderland.

Further away is the Wonnangatta-Moroka unit of the park. Entry from the north-east is by 4WD, but for hikers with 2WDs the western side offers access through Licola and the Howitt road. From a roadside carpark among snow gums it is only about an hour's walk to the Vallejo Ganther Memorial Hut, which lies just off the Alpine Walking Track. I once spent a weekend there with friends who came to carry out some maintenance work on the hut, and I was able to see part of this magnificently wild country. It was December, and on the first night it snowed, lightly dusting the snow gums and the purple carpets of flowering hovea. That these mountains are not to be taken lightly by walkers is evident from some of the place-names: Terrible Hollow, Mount Buggery, Cross Cut Saw, Horrible Gap...

To reach the Cobberas-Tingaringy unit of the park, the quickest way from my home is to drive over the Benambra—Black Mountain road. Although this is closed in winter, and not a desirable road to be on in heavy rain because sections become boggy, I discovered on one trip that the place is fantastic in fog, full of mood and mystery. Some of the State's finest stands of snow and brittle gum grow here, and when enveloped in mist they look quite haunting. On another visit, I made the most of the sunny weather to walk up the Cobberas track, leaving the van in a clearing by the road. Elsewhere it was a hot summer's day but here it was deliciously cool. After walking for about four kilometres through eucalypt woodland I came out onto an alpine meadow full of wildflowers: there were daisies, groundsel, bluebells, and in one part a small spread of exquisite alpine pimeleas. Beyond the meadow lay tantalizing glimpses of the rocky slopes of Mount Cobberas. Unfortunately there wasn't time to go up there, so after dallying a while in the meadow I returned to the car.

View towards Mount Feathertop, summer
Snow gum laden with snow, Bogong High Plains

VICTORIA

Brittle gums (*Eucalyptus mannifera*) in mist, Benambra−Black Mountain road

Razorback Ridge and Mount Feathertop in winter

Near Mount Howitt

VICTORIA

# MOUNT BUFFALO

This park is always the first place to which I take visitors in my district, but it wasn't until some well-travelled friends from overseas marvelled at its unique character that I realized just how special it is. One of the oldest national parks in Australia, Mount Buffalo rises abruptly to 1723 metres over the Ovens, Buckland and Buffalo valleys in eastern Victoria. Its massive vertical granite walls, so loved by hang-gliders, are topped by a plateau littered with rocky outcrops and monstrous granite tors that nestle among snow gums and rear over alpine meadows. In winter, when the gums are stiff with ice and the boulders cheerily wear white caps of snow or perhaps turn into fantastically shaped snowy mounds, it is indeed an unforgettable place.

The plateau in winter

# GRAMPIANS

This imposing national park, with its folded sandstone ranges marked with precipitous bluffs, striking landforms and important Aboriginal rock-art sites, lies 460 kilometres from Melbourne in western Victoria. Even more renowned than its scenery are its wildflowers, as this area is one of Australia's richest floral regions and harbours more than 800 different plants — about one-third of the State's whole indigenous flora. It is thought that the abundance of floral wealth here is due to the fact that the area provided a natural bridge for plants during an age when the rest of the continent was undergoing geological upheavals.

This is one place where visitors may see koalas — and if they don't see any they are bound to hear the males at night making their extraordinary calls, which remind me of a noisy motorbike. I once saw one early in the morning by the Mount Difficult road. A group of Japanese tourists had discovered it, so I pulled up behind their small bus and joined the brigade of excited travellers, all with their cameras aimed at a large koala clinging to a slender treetrunk close to the road. Looking faintly surprised but unperturbed by all the commotion, it peered down at us for quite a few minutes before losing interest and climbing into the treetop. The Japanese were ecstatic.

Common heath (*Epacris impressa*)
Koala

View from Boroka Lookout, Mount Difficult road

# LITTLE DESERT

'The desert that isn't' has long been a common catchphrase to describe the Little Desert, situated to the south of the Western Highway between Dimboola and Kaniva in Victoria's Wimmera district. Its sandy soil was the reason why it was originally called a desert, but that is where the similarity ends. The best time to visit is in spring, when the mallee scrub becomes a wild flowering garden. Some people might say there is nothing to see here, but you will generally find that they have driven through it at 100 kilometres an hour on one of the sealed roads that connect farming communities. This is a place where it is essential to get out of the car and walk through the bush, camp in it, take time to absorb its atmosphere, and notice details of its plants and animals.

I once had the privilege of watching at close hand a malleefowl working at its nesting-mound. The male builds a large mound of sand and brush-litter up to a metre and a half high and five metres in diameter, and then digs an egg-chamber in the top of the mound where the female lays her eggs. Heat for incubation is produced by solar energy and decomposing plant material; a temperature of 33°C is maintained largely by the male as he heaps material on to the mound, or opens it up. Of the 19 species of mound-building birds in the world, the remarkable malleefowl is the only one living in semi-arid conditions.

Malleefowl

# HATTAH-KULKYNE

Situated in virgin mallee country between Mildura and Ouyen in north-west Victoria, the main feature of this park is the Hattah Lakes system, a string of lakes and billabongs fed by periodic flooding from the Murray River. This leafy oasis, where large river red gums shade the edges of the lakes, sustains an abundance of wildlife and provides breeding-grounds for many waterbirds. However, the sand-ridges that run through the area are a reminder of the surrounding mallee scrub's harshness — at Lake Mournpool, dunes lie quite close to the lake.

I was pleased when I learnt that the old sandy track out to Lake Mournpool had been upgraded so that 2WDs could have access without getting bogged, as on an earlier visit the loose sand had caused consider-able difficulties for my van. But when I arrrived at the park to take the nine-kilometre drive out to the lake, I found that the track had been temporarily closed due to heavy flooding.

Dune near Lake Mournpool

# CRADLE MOUNTAIN - LAKE ST CLAIR

This national park has some of the grandest alpine scenery in Australia, but often it is reluctant to reveal its beauty because of the climate. The park's brochures warn people to expect wind, rain and cold; even in summer, snow and severe storms can quickly move in. Visitors may spend days at Cradle Mountain and not even see its distinctive shape, but when the clouds lift — or even partially lift — the sight is breathtaking. Situated in the central Tasmanian highlands, 85 kilometres from Devonport, this national park has two main areas for visitors: Cradle Valley in the north and Lake St Clair in the south. In Cradle Valley, walking-tracks radiate from Waldheim and the Dove Lake carpark; at Lake St Clair they start from the camping ground. The two places are linked by the 80-kilometre Overland Track walking-trail.

This park must not be taken lightly by visitors, and over the years inclement weather has claimed a number of lives. It is essential that even day walkers register their route with rangers — and then stick to it. Failure to do so could lead to trouble, as it once nearly did for me. I had already waited nine days for the weather to clear at Cradle Mountain in order to photograph along the Face Track. Finally, the cold March morning dawned clear with a cloudless sky. After registering my walk in the Day Walk book, I set off. By the time I reached Marions Lookout a few clouds had appeared but I didn't worry, and after looking at the map I decided to take a side track up to Cradle Peak.

For a while the steep track to the peak was well defined, but then it disappeared into a tangled mass of granite boulders, with the route marked by red blobs of paint on the rocks. Gradually the boulders grew bigger and gaps between them opened out to expose large caverns below; a slip causing a fall into one of those holes could be disastrous, as many were too deep for a lone person to get out of without help. I reached what at first looked like a summit, only to find that it was a valley filled with more tumbled boulders. In this grey granite world giant tors reared to the sky, some upright, others leaning forward as they balanced precariously on rock pedestals. I crossed this chaotic Stonehenge and climbed into yet another bouldered valley — it was taking much longer to reach the top than I had thought, and the increasing cloud, although high, had turned a threatening grey. When I eventually stood at the top, the views were stunning. But the weather was anything but: to the south heavy black clouds were swiftly marching towards the peak. I returned over the boulders to the formed track below, casually looked back to where I had just been, and was horrified to see the peak and much of the bouldered slope wrapped in thick cloud. If I had still been up there I would have been in serious trouble, for the red blobs on the boulders were not close together, and it would have been perilously easy to get lost in the fog on that vast sea of rocks. It was then that I realized I hadn't registered this detour in the Day Walk book: not a soul knew I was out on that lonely Peak Track...

Hounslow Heath, near Cradle Mountain
Weindorfers myrtle–beech forest

TASMANIA

Cradle Mountain and Dove Lake

Early-morning mist, Lake St Clair

Shadow Lake, near Lake St Clair

# SOUTHWEST

Covering the far-south-west corner of Tasmania, this park, together with Cradle Mountain - Lake St Clair and Franklin - Lower Gordon Wild Rivers national parks, forms a part of Tasmania's World Heritage Area. By far the largest of the three is Southwest, a wilderness of jagged mountains, glacial lakes, high and often swampy buttongrass plains, and thick vegetation — including the notorious horizontal scrub. There are no roads running through the park and only those who are prepared to walk — often for days — manage to see it properly; in fact, with its bad weather and extremely rugged terrain, this place is said to be the most difficult and challenging in Australia for bushwalkers. Only experienced and well-equipped hikers should attempt the long walks.

However, for motorists it is possible to drive to the edge of the park and look at its magnificent scenery, which forms the backdrop to Lake Pedder. The lake itself is not part of the park, but most of the country bordering its shores south of the Strathgordon area is in it. My favourite part is at the end of the Scotts Peak Dam road, where the Western Arthur Range, a major feature of the park, can be seen to good advantage. The road ends at a high lookout which gives excellent views of the range and Lake Pedder; from here sunrises can be especially memorable, with an early-morning mist often enhancing the effect. I once drove to the lookout in thick fog, but when I arrived at the top it was clear and the sun was just beginning to rise over the range. Below me lay a vast, fleecy sea of mist which turned a delicate shade of pink as the first rays of sun glanced over the mountain, and then, in the strengthening light, gradually whitened to a dazzling brilliance. Quite suddenly the mist lifted, leaving behind veils of gossamer floating over the valleys at the foot of the Western Arthur Range.

From the Scotts Peak Dam road there is access by foot to Mount Anne, another important feature in the park. Many people are content to walk only on its lower slopes for a few hours, as some of the higher parts are extremely difficult. On my first visit I camped at the Mount Anne carpark because there was no other suitable place. But once night fell I did not enjoy it: for some inexplicable reason, whenever I left the cosiness of the van to venture outside I felt uneasy, as if there were 'presences' — and not nice ones — around. On the first night I put it down to the dark windy evening: heavy clouds obliterated the stars, and Mount Anne, partially shrouded in mist, seemed to loom menacingly over the carpark. When daylight came, all the spookiness of the night before seemed nonsensical; after all, I had stayed alone in the bush many times in far more extreme conditions without feeling uneasy. The trouble was, on every night I camped there, including several occasions a few weeks later, there was that same uneasy atmosphere, even when the nights were cloudless. By the 1980s the park rangers had set up a number of camping grounds elsewhere, and it wasn't necessary for me to spend any more nights at Mount Anne.

Western Arthur Range and Lake Pedder
Horizontal scrub

TASMANIA

Western Arthur Range, from Red Knoll Lookout

# ROCKY CAPE

One of Tasmania's smallest national parks, Rocky Cape lies on the north-west coast and stretches for 12 kilometres between Boat Harbour, near Wynyard, and Rocky Cape. The park protects a wildly rugged coastline, small sheltered beaches, heath and wooded hills, and some notable caves. There are two access-roads: the one in the east leads to Sisters Beach from the Boat Harbour Beach road, while that in the west runs for five kilometres from the Bass Highway to Rocky Cape. Walking-tracks within the park link the two places.

I discovered the park during a visit on which I had plenty of time to explore this corner of Tasmania. Its name sounded promising so I went to the west end first, which in my view is the better. At Burgess Bay many colourful rocks provided good subjects for the camera, and there was a ten-minute walk to South Cave, one of several in the park that were first inhabited by Aborigines about 8000 years ago. The views of the craggy coastline from the lighthouse perched high on Rocky Cape were impressive — but the same did not apply to the road up to it, which was a horror; so I left the van at the bottom of the hill and walked up.

Burgess Bay

# FREYCINET

It is surprising how many people travel the 31 kilometres from Tasmania's east-coast highway to the popular coastal resort of Coles Bay, then fail to drive one kilometre further to Freycinet National Park. Even if there is no time to do the rewarding walk to view Wineglass Bay from the saddle between the Hazards' granite-studded Mount Amos and Mount Mayson, a few minutes' drive leads to scenic Sleepy Bay and the fine panorama of the park's east coast that unfolds from the lighthouse. Declared a national park as far back as 1916, Freycinet covers the southern portion of Freycinet Peninsula — a slim finger of land jutting into the Tasman Sea — and all of Schouten Island, lying off its tip.

Sleepy Bay

# Hartz Mountains

Situated 84 kilometres south-west of Hobart, this highland park, with its easy access via Geeveston in the Huon Valley, is an ideal place for day walking. The road winds up to a high plateau reaching 1253 metres at Hartz Peak. Like all of Tasmania's high country, the plateau is subject to sudden changes in weather: snow can fall at any time. Because of the park's altitude, one guidebook recommends visiting it only between November and March, and it was with some trepidation that I decided to spend a night there in late autumn. (To add to my anxiety, on the way up the mountain I realized that the van had no anti-freeze in the radiator.) I needn't have worried: the morning dawned unusually mild. At the Waratah Lookout I photographed the superb panorama of rolling forested ranges and lakes of mist that veiled many of the valleys. Later I walked to Lake Perry and delighted in the distinctly alpine wilderness atmosphere that enveloped the place. The lake nestled beside a boulder-studded range which would have reflected sharply in the lake in still conditions, but to my disappointment a light breeze continually ruffled the water.

From Waratah Lookout

# LINCOLN

This national park lies at the extreme south-eastern tip of Eyre Peninsula, near Port Lincoln. Before visiting it, I contacted the ranger at the park's office in Port Lincoln. 'The best scenery is in the south,' he advised, 'but the Memory Cove track is only for four-wheel-drive vehicles.' When I expressed disappointment at the 4WD access, he suggested that I go to Wanna on the western side, but warned that the road was rough. He was right: it was indeed a rough 10 kilometres, but I took it very slowly and the van coped well enough. Just before reaching the end of the road, I came to a vast expanse of sand which peaked in a high dune. The sand was marked with a maze of wheeltracks, a few of them evidently trying to reach the dune's higher slopes. I walked to the top and away from the intrusive tracks and viewed a

great stretch of pristine sandhills that rolled to the sea. By the time I got to the road's end at the edge of a high cliff, it was near sunset. The best views of the cliff-lined bay, now tinted gold in the last light, lay to the south, and it was easy enough to walk over the rather rough terrain to see them.

The next day I explored the north of the park. Good roads led to pleasant coves where the outgoing tide had left pools of water in the sand which from the hilltops resembled broderie-anglaise patterns. In contrast to the coastal views was Pillie Lake, a small sea of salt lying near the road. I walked out to it but didn't get very far: the ground underneath was moist, and each step I took increased the size and weight of my shoes as a gooey mixture of salt and mud stuck to the soles like thick pancakes.

Pillie Lake

Cliffs at sunset, near Wanna

# NARACOORTE CAVES

Naracoorte Caves Conservation Park is situated about 15 kilometres from the town of Naracoorte in the far south-east of South Australia. The National Parks and Wildlife Service has opened three of the ninety-six documented caves to the general public for inspection: the Alexandra, the Blanche, and the Victoria Fossil. Rangers conduct tours through them at regular intervals, and speleologists can obtain permits to enter many of the others.

These important caves were discovered in the middle of the nineteenth century (on one occasion a dray and an unsuspecting team of bullocks fell into a cave when their weight proved too much for its roof). But properly organized tours did not get under way until the 1970s. The most exciting discovery was in 1968, when a group of exploring speleologists found in a chamber of the Victoria Fossil Cave an extraordinarily rich bed of fossils, which included the bones of many extinct marsupials and other animals, some of them quite large.

For sheer beauty, I found the Alexandra Cave—a wet or 'live' cave—the best: one of its appealing features was the fine display of straw stalagmites and stalactites which in some of the chambers reflected perfectly in still pools of water.

Alexandra Cave

# INNES

Although a favourite with South Australians, Innes National Park is not well known interstate. This is mostly because of its isolated position at the extreme southern tip (often called the 'toe') of Yorke Peninsula; for people travelling across the State on Highway 1, a round-trip detour of about 500 kilometres is required.

The discovery of the rare western whipbird in 1965 may have been the prime reason for establishing the park, but the coastal scenery alone, with its sweeping sandy beaches, high cliffs and bold headlands, is worthy of national-park status. For years the greatest drawcard has been the wreck of the barque *Ethel*, which was driven on to the beach during a gale in 1904. Up till 1988 its great rusted hulk, wearing a hint of mystery and even romance, stood defiantly on the sand, the rugged cliffs providing a dramatic backdrop. I saw it first in 1979, and on returning a decade later I was quite shocked to see from the clifftop only a heap of rusted rubbish: a severe storm, combined with a king tide, had caused it to disintegrate. I was sad it had gone, for somehow its distinctive shape had stirred the imagination. But the splendid beach still deserves a visit, even though it's a bit of a scramble down the steep rough path from the carpark — the most tricky part being to find the safest access-point from the clifftop without tumbling over its edge.

Wreck of the *Ethel*

The *Ethel* wreck after 1988

# MOUNT REMARKABLE

Lying across the southern Flinders Ranges south of Port Augusta and Wilmington, this national park has two points of entry: Mambray Creek on the western side and Alligator Gorge in the east. For many years camping was permitted at Mambray Creek, but since the mid-1980s a more formal camp with numbered bush sites has been available. Over the years, when passing through the area I have found Mambray Creek a more pleasant overnight stop than Port Augusta, 45 kilometres away. Situated only a few minutes off the highway, the camping ground is shaded by huge old river red gums, and there is some good walking along the tracks that lead up the gorge and over the hills, with sweeping views over the range.

Mambray Creek

# FLINDERS RANGES

Located approximately 450 kilometres north of Adelaide, Flinders Ranges National Park is one of South Australia's major and best-loved parks. It protects some of the finest scenery found in the 400-kilometre-long Flinders Ranges, covering much of the central region, from Wilpena Pound in the south to just beyond Aroona Valley in the north, and from the Heysen Range in the west to The Bunkers with Wilkawillana Gorge in the east. This area, with its majestic river red gums, its carpets of spring wild-flowers, and the colour and incredible contours of the rugged hills, peaks and mountains (subject to such superb changes of light at sunrise and sunset), has long been a source of inspiration for artists and photographers, and a favourite with campers, bush-walkers and motorists. Indeed, the country between Wilpena and Aroona has even been declared 'the loveliest twenty miles in Australia'!

Wilpena Pound is probably the best-known place of the entire Flinders. Eleven kilometres long, and nearly five kilometres wide across its middle portion, the Pound is shaped like an immense amphitheatre; from the air it resembles a great mountainous dish. The only access into it is via a gap through which Wilpena Creek flows. Near this entrance are a camp-ing ground and chalet, which provide a good base for exploring the Pound and much of the park. There are some fine walks in the Pound but, as in the rest of the Flinders Ranges, the walking can be physically de-manding, especially in hot weather, since many of the tracks pass over some extremely rough ground without water.

If I'm not walking in the Pound I prefer to camp elsewhere in the park, a favourite place being Brachina Gorge. This long and wildly beautiful gorge, which once had many bullock-wagons pass by its towering cliffs, lies in the Heysen Range just south of Aroona Valley. The most scenic approach to it is by way of Bunyeroo Valley and Gorge, but don't attempt it after heavy rain, as the creeks will be in spate and the road slippery. Brachina Gorge also is not a good place to be during rain, because flooded creeks stop most 2WDs — as I once bitterly discovered. The weather had been fine so I decided to camp in the gorge; but that night some 50 millimetres of rain fell, and the creek that cut the road in many places had changed from a shallow trickling stream to a deep raging torrent. The forecast was for more rain, and I had very little food left. As I didn't fancy the idea of living on a starvation diet until the road conditions improved, I decided to have a go at getting out later that day. After what can only be described as a nightmare drive through flooded creeks and boggy sections of the track, I reached the Leigh Creek bitumen road just as the heavens opened and released more torrential rain. I now always make sure I have plenty of emergency food rations whenever I camp in Brachina Gorge.

Brachina Gorge

Bunyeroo Gorge

The Pound Range, from Bunyeroo Lookout

# FLINDERS CHASE

This park on Kangaroo Island offers a feast of good coastal scenery, as some of South Australia's finest coastline is found along the shores of the island, which lies off Fleurieu Peninsula. Nowadays there is easy vehicular access by a ferry that takes about an hour to cross Backstairs Passage between Cape Jervis and Penneshaw; this is a vast improvement on the tedious eight-hour journey that used to be necessary from Port Adelaide to Kingscote.

The national park protects a large portion of the island's western end, and features two well-known landforms: Remarkable Rocks and Admiral Arch. Both are easy to reach. Remarkable Rocks, a collection of weirdly shaped granite boulders balancing on a domed granite headland, lie near Cape du Couedic. It is not enough to view the rocks from the carpark: you should take a walk among these unusual formations that resemble broken eggshells, huge claws and sculptor's clay (before and after an artisan has been at work). The Arch, a huge open cave through which the Southern Ocean's powerful waves can be seen lashing the rocks, lies in the cliffs at Cape du Couedic. My favourite time to see it is sunset, when the waves and rocks, darkly framed by the cave's great jagged archway, glow warmly in the setting sun.

Remarkable Rocks

Admiral Arch

# ULURU

This important national park, which lies about 450 kilometres south-west of Alice Springs in central Australia, has two of the world's most outstanding natural wonders: Ayers Rock, a colossal piece of weathered sandstone, and the Olgas, a collection of extraordinary domes set in a circle, just west of Ayers Rock. Although the Rock is geologically distinct from the Olgas, both formations are sandstone and each is the revealed surface of a huge parent rock buried in the sandy plain. Both places are sacred symbols of the Aboriginal Dreamtime legends.

The base for seeing the park is Yulara, built 20 kilometres from Ayers Rock in the 1980s for the express purpose of providing facilities for the growing number of tourists who come here. Many people lament the changes that have taken place at Uluru. In the pre-Yulara days, when the camping ground lay in the shadow of the Rock, just a kilometre away, who could forget the fantastic sight of the great brooding monolith lighting up at sunrise? Today that area is closed to the public, and although many visitors drive out to see the sunrise from the new bitumen road encircling the Rock, the scenic angle is not as good as the one from the old camping ground.

Both the Rock and the Olgas are renowned for their superb colour-effects, caused by vagaries of the weather and the play of light. Throughout the day they can change from soft shades of mauve to deeper browns and pinks; and at sunrise and sunset they glow red, the brilliance of colour being determined by the amount of dust in the air and the position and density of the clouds. It is this brilliance at sunset which can be a highlight of a visit. Every evening the area known as Sunset Strip is packed with cars and coaches, and hundreds of people take up positions on the plain and gaze expectantly at the Rock, cameras clutched in readiness to capture that brief moment when it will flare red. Another highlight is to climb its 348-metre heights. Everyone seems to want to attempt it, regardless of age (an 89-year-old man has reached the top) or suitability of dress (I have seen women in tight skirts and high heels on the slopes) — in spite of the fact that it is difficult and, if you stray from the white line, dangerous. The record number of climbs made by one person in a day is said to be 27, though most people who have climbed the Rock will wonder why anyone would want to do it more than once.

In many ways I prefer the Olgas to Ayers Rock. Their weatherworn shapes are a delight to explore and to photograph. The view from the top of Katajuta — the only dome that is easy and safe to climb — presents one of Australia's most stunning landscapes, especially in the early-morning light when all the domes across the valley are a vibrant pink. Walking in the Olgas' ravines (such as the Valley of the Winds and Mount Olga Gorge), you will see the rough conglomerate walls studded with a million varieties of pebbles; and it is a strange sensation to look up at the tops of the sheer high walls, which almost threaten to topple over everything. Whenever I walk in these ravines I keep a watchful eye for perenties, Australia's largest goannas: back in the 1970s, one of the park rangers sighted a huge one whose body was estimated to be as thick as a man's thigh — an exceptional size for a perentie.

Ayers Rock

NORTHERN TERRITORY

The Olgas at sunset

Moonset over the Olgas

# ORMISTON GORGE AND POUND

This national park protects Ormiston Pound and one of the most spectacular gorges in the MacDonnell Ranges, which extend for many kilometres both east and west of Alice Springs in central Australia. Ormiston Gorge lies in the western ranges, and is linked to Alice Springs by 134 bitumen kilometres. To appreciate the full grandeur of this place you need to walk through the gorge to the pound so as to see at close hand the awe-inspiring reddish walls, splashed with colours of white, yellow, vermilion, grey, black and brown, that rise to heights of 200 metres. If there is plenty of water around, the scenes can be breathtaking—especially by the long pool at the entrance to the gorge, only a few minutes' walk from the camping ground and carpark.

Ormiston Gorge

# FINKE GORGE

Situated near Hermannsburg, some 140 kilometres south-west of Alice Springs, this park features two of the Centre's most famous places: Palm Valley, with its ancient Livistona palms, relics of a wetter age when the region was covered with tropical vegetation; and the nearby Amphitheatre, an unusual semicircular range displaying eroded headlands, spires and bluffs. Access is only by 4WD, because once it reaches the Finke Gorge the track runs along the sandy bed of the Finke River, and the last section into Palm Valley is over rocky terrain. But so popular is this park that visitors without suitable transport will have no trouble booking one of the many commercial day tours that operate from Alice Springs. If you are visiting Alice and have time only for one day of sightseeing, I would suggest a trip to Palm Valley, as the route is packed with good scenery. Once in Palm Valley, a delightful walk over wide expanses of flat rock will take you past rockpools reflecting palms and cycads, fallen boulders and colourful chunky cliffs. If you can spend the night in this park, don't miss seeing the Amphitheatre from the Initiation Rock lookout at sunset.

The Amphitheatre

# KAKADU

Almost as soon as it was declared a national park in 1979, Kakadu became one of the country's most important reserves, and within a decade had been accepted for inclusion on the World Heritage List. Covering an immense area and located at the top of the Northern Territory, about 250 kilometres east of Darwin at the edge of Arnhem Land, Kakadu is special not only because it preserves a wealth of wildlife, scenic beauty and natural features (almost the entire drainage basin of the great South Alligator River lies within the park), but also because of its rich heritage of Aboriginal culture.

Much of its beauty lies in its tropical wetlands, a unique world comprising vast floodplains, rivers, lagoons, channels and billabongs, which are fed by the heavy monsoonal rains that drench the region between November and April. This area abounds in wildlife and is comparable to the world's great wildlife reserves. On one memorable occasion Toby Gangali, a ranger and one of the Aboriginal traditional owners of Kakadu, took me to a place called Goose Camp, where the lagoon, alive with masses of birds, resembled some kind of giant aviary. I could hardly believe my eyes at the sight of so many egrets, herons, ducks and stilts, yet their numbers paled in comparison with the honking hordes of magpie geese among them.

In contrast to the wetlands is the worn and craggy Arnhem Land escarpment, a dominant feature in the east of the park. In many places the escarpment's sandstone cliffs are notched with deep, narrow gorges that are at their most impressive during the wet season, when the rains give rise to thundering waterfalls that pour over sheer rocky walls. One of the most notable is the Jim Jim Falls. The edge of the escarpment has also been eroded by streams, causing a variety of rocky outliers to be left isolated on the plains, such as Nourlangie Rock, Jabiru Dreaming and Ubirr. In the overhanging shelters of these outliers lie galleries of Aboriginal rock art, recognized as the finest of their type. Because they present a vital record of human occupation of the area, these galleries are extremely important to the present-day owners of the land, many of whom still have traditional association with the paintings. At Nourlangie Rock an excellent boardwalk has been erected to enable visitors to view the art easily, while providing protection for it as well.

Like Uluru, Kakadu has undergone many changes in recent years because of the great volume of people visiting it. This has resulted in a high degree of organization — and in restrictions that many find disappointing. Others think that the park is being taken over by commercial tours. Certainly one gets that impression at Yellow Water Lagoon: on my last visit I noted that when the boat tours returned at the end of the day, the skippers, instead of stopping a short distance upstream to show passengers the sunset, moved their boats into positions just opposite the carpark and effectively blocked for other visitors one of the best sunset scenes in the park. I'm glad I have memories of Yellow Water before this started happening.

Ubirr

Early morning, Sandy Billabong

Brumbies in the mist, at sunrise
Magpie geese and water-whistle ducks

NORTHERN TERRITORY

Sunset over Yellow Water Lagoon

# NITMILUK

In 1989 Katherine Gorge National Park changed its name to Nitmiluk when it was handed back to the Aboriginal traditional owners. Although it is only a part of the park, Katherine Gorge is the main attraction, and its boat tours have long been considered a 'must' for anyone visiting the top of the Northern Territory. Situated near the town of Katherine, 312 kilometres south of Darwin, this great cleft in the southernmost reaches of the Arnhem Plateau comprises thirteen gorges that imprison the Katherine River between high cliffs. There are only two ways to see the gorges from the ground: by walking over the clifftops, and by boat.

Those who want to escape the tourist crowds around the busy caravan park and on the equally busy boat tours can find peace either by exploring the gorges in a hired canoe or by walking to the various clifftop lookouts and spots by the river that offer safe swimming. If you choose to walk, I recommend doing it as early as possible in the day in order to avoid the heat; also, at that time the colours of the land are richer, and the tropical woodland and rocky gullies through which the paths pass are bathed in a delicious freshness that vanishes as soon as the sun climbs high in the sky. There is more good walking at Edith Falls, reached by a five-day walk from Katherine Gorge, or by the bitumen access-road off the Stuart Highway between Katherine and Pine Creek.

Edith Falls

Katherine Gorge

# KEEP RIVER

Lying just off the Victoria Highway in the north-west corner of the Northern Territory by the Western Australian border, this park is becoming increasingly popular with visitors en route to the Kimberley. Its main attraction is the highly eroded terrain, which features bluffs, ridges, and formations like those in the Kimberley's Bungle Bungle Range; indeed, this park is sometimes referred to as a 'mini-Bungles'. At the Gurrandalng picnic and camping ground, situated about 15 kilometres into the park, there is a rewarding four-kilometre walk that winds over and down a dissected ridge backing on to a towering cliff, and on the loop back to the carpark passes through some 'beehive' formations like those in the Bungle Bungle Range. This walk is at its best in the late afternoon, when it is cooler and there is a wonderful light on the sandstone.

Further north in the park is Keep River Gorge. It is possible to walk about five kilometres into the gorge, and the further you go the better the scenery becomes. Another activity I thoroughly enjoyed was the time spent birdwatching from a hide built into the base of a windmill overlooking Cockatoo Lagoon, near the rangers' station.

Gurrandalng

# GREGORY

This national park incorporates part of the Northern Territory's most important river, the Victoria, which rises in the spinifex plains of the Great Sandy Desert and flows for about 640 kilometres before it empties its wide waters into Joseph Bonaparte Gulf on the Territory's north-west coast. For motorists who have made the journey along the Victoria Highway from Katherine through 195 kilometres of open and rather uninteresting tropical woodland, the scenery of the Victoria River Valley in this section of the park is most refreshing. Boat trips on the river are sometimes available from the caravan park situated by the highway.

Victoria River

# BUNGLE BUNGLE

The Bungle Bungle Range is one of Australia's most extraordinary landscapes. Just as extraordinary is the fact that until its 'discovery' by an aerial film crew in 1983 only the Aborigines and some pastoralists knew it existed in the remote country lying between Kununurra and Halls Creek in the Kimberley. By 1987 this geological masterpiece had been declared a national park. Rising from the plains as a great triangular massif, the range is cut by ravines and edged by high cliffs that in places reach 400 metres and give way to a myriad weathered orange-and-black-banded domes; it is these beehive-like formations that visitors come to see.

Called Pernululu by the Aborigines, 'the Bungles' lie 300 kilometres by road from Kununurra and about half that distance from Halls Creek. Many people see the range only from the air; in fact, that exhilarating flight has become an important item on the tourist itinerary. Soon after the world knew of the place, the inevitable 4WD track was pushed through to its edge. The initial track was not for the fainthearted, but by 1988 it took only about four hours of hard driving to cover the 55 kilometres from the highway to the Piccaninny Gorge area. By the following year more work had been done on the road, reducing the time to about three hours with little risk of wrecking your car. But the route is still strictly 4WD and is likely to remain so for many years. Since my campervan was not 4WD, I had to rely on commercial safaris to show me the Bungles.

The best area to see the 'beehives' is around Piccaninny Creek, at the southern end of the range. The last few kilometres pass through outcrops of domes which, as you approach the massif, appear as part of it, in places displaying multitudes of little hills piled high upon each other. The track normally poses no problem for drivers, but on my last visit a grader had just been through and had turned the firm but corrugated track into a stretch of fine loose sand which provided difficulties for many visitors. One badly bogged vehicle blocked our way in: the driver had forgotten to engage his hubs for the 4WD mode — apparently one of the commonest causes of a 4WD getting bogged!

From the carpark it was a short walk to Piccaninny Creek, which runs for about six kilometres before entering Piccaninny Gorge. We explored only around its entrance; for safety reasons, walkers planning to go right through must register the walk with the rangers because it is possible to get lost in the numerous side gorges. One of these, the stately Cathedral Gorge, lies close to the carpark so we were able to walk in to it.

A fascinating gorge that visitors may see is Echidna Chasm, situated on the north-western side of the range, near Kurrajong camping ground. This narrow ravine sees little sun, but the walls glow a warm red and make a perfect backdrop for the dark shapes of the many ancient Livistona palms growing there. Dead fronds crackle underfoot as you make your way for about thirty minutes through the chasm, which narrows to a metre before ending abruptly at a great wall of rock.

Echidna Chasm and the Piccaninny Gorge area were the only two places open to the public during my visits.

Piccaninny Creek

Livistona palms, Echidna Chasm

Aerial view of 'beehive' domes

WESTERN AUSTRALIA

# WINDJANA GORGE

For sheer grandeur Windjana Gorge is the most impressive of all the well-known gorges in the Kimberley region of Western Australia, and this small national park has long been a favourite with visitors. Situated 150 kilometres from Derby and carved over the centuries by the floodwaters of the Lennard River, the gorge runs for about five kilometres through the limestone Napier Range. Although many people travelling from the east take the back road to Windjana from Fitzroy Crossing, motorists with caravans will find that access is much easier from Derby because the other way is twisty and rough.

I love this place because every time I visit it some other marvellous aspect is revealed. Within the gorge's first kilometre before it turns sharply east, there is a sense of space which in no way lessens the splendour of the orange-splashed grey walls that rise like a mighty fortress to 90 metres above the plain.

Take a walk and quietly absorb the beauty of your surroundings: it is early morning and the gorge is partially flooded with a soft translucent light that barely lifts the veils of shadow clinging to the cliffs.

Some clouds start to drift in from the west, but there is no wind and the clouds together with the gorge's great walls are deeply mirrored in the long pools of water. In the nearby trees a large flock of noisy corellas festoon the branches like white cottonwool. As you pass the pool by the great white rock, you see what appear to be some straight nobbly logs floating on the surface; they will be the harmless Johnstone's freshwater crocodiles, so used to people quietly walking past that they don't even submerge completely. Later, on the way back, you spot one lying on the bank sunbaking, and standing companionably beside it is a white egret. But this delightful scene is brief, for suddenly the egret wings its graceful way over the pool and just as quickly the crocodile slides into the water to join the other floating 'logs'. Then, as if to welcome you back to your camp, there is a sudden vivid flashing of pink against the grey ramparts of the gorge, and a mob of screeching galahs wheel in the air, their raucous cries echoing loudly around the range. Despite the noise, there is a deep feeling of peace.

Windjana Gorge

# HAMERSLEY RANGE

For people who live in south-eastern Australia, the Hamersley Range is one of the hardest places to reach, because of the distance involved and the travelling time required. However, it is worth every moment of the long drive. Situated in the north-west of Western Australia, some 1450 kilometres north of Perth and about 900 kilometres south-west of the Kimberley, this iron-ore-rich range is a major feature of the hot dry Pilbara region. Because it is ironstone country, the unsealed roads are among the stoniest in Australia. It is also one of the worst places for dust: fine and rust-coloured, it gets into everything and leaves you feeling permanently grubby—even after washing—because everything you touch seems to be coated with it.

Hamersley Range National Park protects only a section of this vast range. Its main attractions are the colourful gorges fissuring the plateau that tops it. From Wittenoom, roads lead up to the plateau, to the camping grounds, and to the sheer gorges that reveal terraced walls of chocolate, red and rusty browns; these vivid colours are accentuated by the white trunks of snappy gums and the lush vegetation beside the pools of water lying deep in the gorges. If it is spring, a host of bright-hued wildflowers add to the brilliance of the scene.

Although it is possible to go down into some of the gorges (one of the roads to the plateau runs through Yampire Gorge), most people prefer to view them from the top. Paths lead to good vantage-points, but when you wander away from them loose stones can become treacherous underfoot. Most of the gorges are 'musts' to visit. At Dales Gorge there are fine views from the clifftops, and an easy path leads down to the Fortescue Falls and a large pool. There are other grand views at Gordon Oxer Lookout, where Joffre, Red, Hancock and Weano gorges meet. But the most dramatic—and terrifying—is the panorama over Knox and Red gorges from the clifftop lookout at the end of a 600-metre walking-track by Knox Gorge. Here the perpendicular walls plunge to around 150 metres, and as at all the other viewing areas, there are no guard-rails. Unless I have a camera in my hand, heights usually scare me; but Knox Gorge is one place where even with a camera I feel quite dizzy as I creep uneasily to the edge of that frightful precipice in order to get a better angle for a photograph.

My favourite gorge is Kalamina. It isn't threatening, like some of the grander ones; it is somehow a more intimate place, and with its chunky chocolate-coloured walls, shaded pools and cool vegetation, it epitomizes the essential character of all the gorges. There is easy access from the carpark and some good walking through the gorge. I suspect that many visitors do not see Kalamina properly: all the people I spoke to who had been there had reached only the pool and falls that lie close to the carpark. Admittedly the view downstream from the pool, with some rather untidy vegetation, isn't particularly inviting; but after that the gorge quickly reveals its beauty.

Knox Gorge

Kalamina Gorge
Snappy gum (*Eucalyptus leucophloia*)

# MILLSTREAM-CHICHESTER

In the 1980s two areas utterly different in character in the West's Pilbara region were incorporated into one national park: Millstream's beautiful pool with the nearby Fortescue River, and the arid Chichester Range. Lying just off the Wittenoom—Roebourne road, the long, lily-covered pool at Millstream, thickly lined with paperbarks and a unique species of *Livistona* palm, wells from a natural spring and flows into the Fortescue River. The river's deep pools are also lined with lush vegetation, and the combination of shade and water (rare commodities in the Pilbara) provides a refreshing antidote for the region's heat and dust. Crossing Pool is my favourite place on the river, and like many people I always end up spending more days here than planned, and then find it extremely hard to break camp.

Once back on the Roebourne road it takes about 45 minutes to drive to the Chichester Range, where the road runs over its top. This is 'painted desert' country: rust and chocolate-hued rocks dominate the scenes, and the ridgetops are so littered with them that it seems as if a huge tiptruck had been at work among the golden spinifex. Some of the richest colour is at Python Pool at the foot of the range, when at sunrise the high rocky walls around the pool blaze briefly as if on fire, spilling red and then orange colours over the water. I've never met any pythons here, but apparently they often used to be seen lying in the pool's cool water.

Millstream

Chichester Range

# CAPE RANGE

Shortly before this book was conceived, the artist Jack Absalom enthusiastically told me to photograph Cape Range the next time I was in the West. It was a place I knew little about, and I had seen no photographs of it. Situated some 1200 kilometres north of Perth, this national park lies near Exmouth on North West Cape, the small peninsula that juts into the Indian Ocean north of Carnarvon. It incorporates the rugged canyon-cleft limestone range from which it is named, and has more than 50 kilometres of pristine-white sandy beaches on the west side of the cape. Immediately offshore is Ningaloo Maritime Park, which protects a superb coral reef.

Much of the range is inaccessible, but two roads on the eastern side give access from the Exmouth road: the Shothole Canyon Road twists for about 12 kilometres along the bottom of a deep gorge, while the Charles Knife Road runs steeply for about 15 kilometres over a razorlike ridge before ending at a capped oilwell. Both roads are suitable for 2WDs, but to cross the range to the coast a 4WD is required — plus a knowledge of where you are going, as the way is not marked.

Not knowing the area, I decided to get an overview of the park by taking a day tour from Exmouth; then I could plan my own exploration in the limited time available. It was a good tour: it visited the canyons, crossed the range, and included a boat trip up Yardie Gorge. The canyons on the eastern side were unlike any others I had seen in Australia. On both sides of the Charles Knife Road colourful chasms yawned open, demonstrating a classic case of massive erosion that had occurred over the ages. The track over the range to the coast passed through some desolate terrain, the only interesting feature we saw being a sinkhole-type cave that had a giant figtree with many metres of dangling roots guarding its entrance.

At Yardie Gorge craggy rust-coloured cliffs line a permanent waterhole in Yardie Creek; a sandbar blocks its entrance to the sea when the creek is not in spate. In a little dinghy we explored this lovely gorge, where we sighted blackbanded wallabies on the gentler slopes and many kinds of birds. Finally we walked along several of the park's beaches, where fine stark-white sand gave way to water a glorious shade of turquoise that in turn changed to a dark inky-blue beyond the reef. Although it was a Sunday, there were few people around and we mostly had the beaches to ourselves — but that is typical of Western Australia, where there is so much space and a relatively small population.

After the tour I returned to Yardie Gorge in my campervan via the coastal road from Exmouth, and walked along the clifftops at sunrise. By far the best walking, both for good scenic views and for negotiating the terrain, was on the southern side of the creek; the northern side was impossibly rough. A couple of other camps were set up near the sandbar when I arrived. When the ranger came to collect the fees, I commented that the park was not very well known in the eastern States. 'That's just as well,' he replied drily. 'We're getting enough people here as it is.'

Yardie Gorge

# NAMBUNG

Until 1986, only people in vehicles with a good clearance could visit the remarkable Pinnacles Desert in Nambung National Park, situated on the coast 250 kilometres north of Perth. The last few kilometres leading to the park from the small village of Cervantes were a horror stretch of monstrous stones; to get over them without wrecking your car required careful navigation and some steady nerves. For years tourist groups had pressured the government to upgrade the track, but others wanted it to remain unchanged as it provided some protection for the desert's fragile environment. However, with the phenomenal increase in 4WD vehicles and the inroads that tourism was making into wilderness areas elsewhere, it was inevitable that the track would be improved. Now a good gravel road is open to all traffic, including coaches.

Lying among the sandy heathlands of the park, the Pinnacles Desert features a vast collection of limestone spires that rise from the bare sands like some kind of weird graveyard or ruined city. When I first visited the place in a Kombi back in 1975, much of the sand was held together by a unique crust that seemed made up of tiny petrified roots only a few centimetres long, some lying on the ground, others valiantly erect like minute icicles. They were so fragile that they disintegrated at the lightest touch. On a recent visit I couldn't find any: much of the sand was covered with masses of footprints.

The Pinnacles

# WALPOLE-NORNALUP

Most visitors exploring the south-west corner of Western Australia will pass through this national park, as it lies by the highway on the south coast, about 110 kilometres west of Albany. The park is renowned for its tranquil inlets, its wildflowers, and some magnificent stands of karri, jarrah and red tingles.

Because of the wildflowers, I always like to visit the south-west in spring. However, although the flowers are usually impressive, the weather often isn't: over the years my visits to this park have always been dogged by miserable rain. But on the final morning of my last visit I saw for the first time the true beauty of Nornalup and Walpole inlets. At first they were heavily veiled in mists, which created a rather wintry effect as the early-morning sun tried to pierce the chilly gloom of the fog; but gradually the mists lifted to reveal reflections that gave an intense depth to many of the scenes along the Knoll Drive, near the Coalmine Beach camping area.

Nornalup Inlet

# FITZGERALD RIVER

For the traveller, Western Australia in spring is full of surprises, and for me one of them was Fitzgerald River National Park, near Hopetoun, 225 kilometres east of Albany. Once, while en route to Esperance, I visited a wildflower show at Ongerup, and one of the attendants recommended this park as being a good place for wildflowers. She suggested a shortcut to the park via West River Road; but as that road soon deteriorated into a track that held distinct promise of being unsuitable for 2WDs, I returned to the highway. Later I learnt that much of the park is accessible only to 4WDs. However, there was no problem with the road into the park from Hopetoun, and the ones around East Mylies and West Mylies beaches were also good.

There is some interesting scenery here, much of it dominated by the Barrens, a system of small ranges and isolated peaks extending over 60 kilometres. I quickly realized I had entered a botanist's paradise, a veritable garden full of the most astonishing variety of wildflowers, with many species endemic to the park. This was banksia country at its best, and I was delighted to find here one of the most intriguing of Australia's 60-odd species: the possum banksia (*Banksia baueri*). Larger than the average banksia flower and wearing a coat that resembled the shaggy fur of an orangutan, it nestled into the foliage like a small animal. Another surprise was the royal hakeas (*Hakea victoriae*), extraordinary plants with variegated leaves which rose in columns to tower over the other vegetation.

Near East Mylies Beach

Royal hakea (*Hakea victoriae*)

# EUCLA

Some of the country's highest coastal dunes are in Eucla National Park, located east of Eucla near the South Australian border, between the Eyre Highway and the lonely shores of the Great Australian Bight. Access to the dunes is from Eucla, five kilometres away. Originally the dunes were anchored by vegetation, but by the end of the 1890s armies of introduced rabbits had reached Eucla and devoured enough of the plant-cover to allow large-scale erosion. Driven by strong winds, these Sahara-like dunes are slowly on the move, and have just about buried the ruins of the old telegraph station that in 1877 provided the first direct link between east and west.

The dunes are marvellous at sunrise and sunset, when the long shadows give a sculpted appearance, creating knife-edged tops that sweep to softly rounded sandhills marked with a sea of undisturbed ripples. Few people appear to explore the dunes beyond the ruins and the track leading to the beach — but then the elements often do not encourage much exploration. Once I was daft enough to attempt a walk in a howling wind: sand stung my legs and crept into my ears, pockets and camera-bag (disaster!), then obliterated all my tracks. Another time, on approaching Eucla from the west during a raging gale, I saw in the distance a strange sight: great clouds of sand glinting in the afternoon sun rose from the dunes and appeared to hang suspended over them. The dunes were in the grip of a fierce sandstorm. On that occasion I did not go down to see them.

Dunes at Eucla

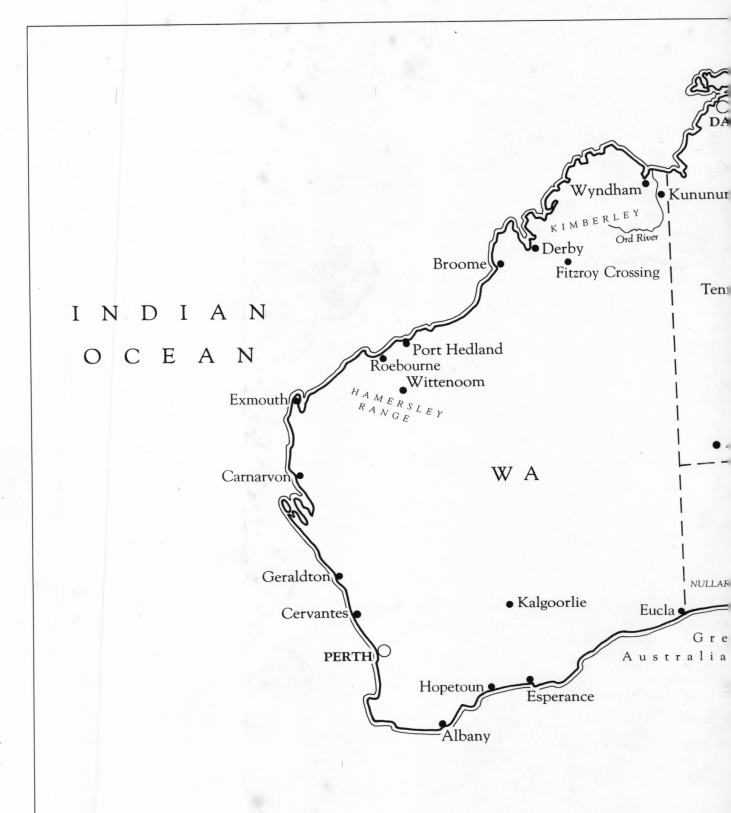